AFTER
THE
WATERGAW

By the same author

The Bird and the Monkey (Highland Printmakers, 1996)
Total Immersion (Scottish Cultural Press, 1998)

Other poetry from Scottish Cultural Press

AFTER
THE
WATERGAW

*a collection of new poetry from Scotland
inspired by water*

edited by

Robert Davidson

SCOTTISH CULTURAL PRESS

First published 1998 by
Scottish Cultural Press
Unit 14, Leith Walk Business Centre,
130 Leith Walk, Edinburgh EH6 5DT
Tel: 0131 555 5950 ◆ Fax: 0131 555 5018
e-mail: scp@sol.co.uk

British Library Cataloguing in Publication Data
A catalogue entry for this book is available from the British Library

ISBN: 1 84017 024 7

The publisher acknowledges a subsidy from the Scottish Arts Council
towards the publication of this book

THE SCOTTISH ARTS COUNCIL

Printed and bound by
Cromwell Press Ltd, Trowbridge, Wiltshire

Contents

Acknowledgements

Many people played a part in the production of this collection. I am grateful to the charity's Highland Committee who, under the chairmanship of William Bruce, gave their enthusiastic support to the idea from its first being mooted. Jill Dick of Scottish Cultural Press adopted the project on first hearing and has been supportive and encouraging through some trying times. My friends Ann and Kerr Yule have, as ever, been aye ready with shoulders to cry on and sage advice.

I am grateful to my employers, the North of Scotland Water Authority, for use of an office computer and software for collation of the poems and for postal services and stationery. Similarly, my colleagues and immediate superiors have all shown exceptional tolerance and I am happy to place my gratitude on record. I am especially grateful to James Hawkins for permission to use his beautiful painting, Old Pine (diptych), (acrylic on canvas), *on the cover, and to Sam Gilliland who first suggested the collection's title. Thanks also to Carol Rodger for her patience and efforts at the Scottish Cultural Press console.*

Above all, of course, I am grateful to the poets whose work is presented in the following pages and who have given of their talents and creativity without recompense or reward. I hope they enjoy this presentation of their work, it is they who have made the project worthwhile. Any views expressed, of course, do not necessarily reflect those of the charity.

A few of the poems have already appeared elsewhere; George Bruce's Velasquez *in* The Scotsman, *Ron Butlin's* Preparations for a Sea Voyage *in* Ragtime in Unfamiliar Bars, *Robert Crawford's* Impossibility, *in its entirety, in* London Review of Books, *Kathleen Jamie's* The Tay Moses *in the American magazine* Columbia, *Peadar Morgan's* A 'Coiseachd Anns An Uisge *first appeared in* Gairm, *Janet Paisley's* Reading The Bones *in* Nomad, *Dilys Rose's* Figurehead *in* Madame Doubtfire's Dilemma. *To any who have been overlooked I apologise.*

For all the volunteers
and for all of their works

Inheriting The Earth

Water is life's most precious resource, without which we would die in only a few days, and yet a quarter of the world's population do not have safe water to drink. All over the Third World people of all ages, but particularly children, are stricken by diseases directly attributable to unsafe water and poor sanitation.

Disease is the most visible and urgent part of the problem. Sadly it is not the only one. Throughout the developing world, women and children use up precious hours and energy collecting and carrying water that is barely sufficient in quantity and quality for their needs. Of course this time could be spent on other work – and on education – were it not for the desperate urgency of thirst. The truth is that everyone in the world needs access to safe water and effective sanitation.

This is not necessarily a simple task. Meeting even basic requirements includes integrating water, sanitation and hygiene activities, using appropriate technologies and keeping costs low. Long term solutions are only likely to be achieved with the active support of the communities involved and with their national and local authorities.

This collection of new Scottish poems inspired by water has been written and collated by the named contributors, so that the royalty payments generated by the collection as a whole can be directed towards these needs through a particular water-oriented charity. However, the charity eventually decided, sadly to my mind, that it should have no formal or contractual association with this book. This is a decision that both the editor and publisher must accept and respect, although, it has to be stated, with very great regret.

The charity's ends and efforts continue to be entirely admirable and wholly laudable and, I feel, are both commended and praised by the quality of the individual contributions and the spirit of the collection as a whole. All royalties from its sale are being donated by the poets towards their furtherance.

In this light I would like to point out that there are many crying needs and many worthwhile causes in this world. Everywhere there are dedicated and self-effacing people giving of themselves freely and anonymously in furtherance of what we might broadly agree to call 'the common good'. The dedication to this book should be read as including them all. Eventually they will inherit the earth.

Robert Davidson
Editor

Water And Scotland

On the wall of the Clan Donald Centre, at Armadale on the Isle of Skye, there is one of those maps that disconcert you by being centred in some unusual way. This one looks down, from a floating location somewhere over Greenland, on the ragged north-western edge of the continent of Europe. The effect is startling to one accustomed to viewing the British Isles as the centre of the world, something like having the Pacific Rim presented as a whole rather than as a collection of fragments from the peripheries of remembered maps. It seems wholeness is as much a perception as a condition.

New worlds of possibility appear as the eye drops from the Arctic Circle, down through Norway and the short crossing to Shetland and Orkney, to the west coast of Scotland, the Hebrides and the west coast of Ireland. It is immediately obvious that there has always been a sort of unity here for those prepared to travel on water, even more so to those dwellers on coastal plains whose inland access was rendered difficult by mountains.

Such a coastline, of innumerable fjords and kyles, will have made long journeys in short stages practical whether the travellers sailed in longboats, birlinn or coracles. Viewed in this way the trip to what is now known as America, making harbours in the Faroes, Iceland and Greenland, seems almost inevitable, not only for Erik and his Vikings but also for Brendan and his monks.

Water, therefore, was the native element for such people and not only for travel. All of their communities lived unshielded from the storms and squalls that swirled over the north Atlantic and burst on them from the west, storms that broke on the mountain ranges behind and returned to them in torrents of fresh water that could be utilised in agriculture and to power mills, and for sanitation. There would have been occasional catastrophic floods.

They would have learned to read the weather and understood its function of transforming and transporting water. They will have understood also that water in all of its many forms, salt and fresh, river and loch, is really just the one water. They cannot but have realised that their many tribes and nations, while also of different forms, were also one. They will have learned to both value and fear the processes of transformation.

However, while these often turbulent processes of intercourse and integration went on other great movements of history were also taking place, and overtaking them, so that the individuated coastal state never came to be. Instead, the Danish and Swedish states, incorporating Norway at different times, and the British state, often known simply as England, were formed. Ireland was violently incorporated into the latter and later, equally violently, withdrew. Mostly. Scotland was absorbed by peaceful means and may yet peacefully withdraw. The European idea seems to run more harmoniously with the Irish and Scottish ideas than with the Scandinavian or British.

The more things change the more they remain the same. The western coastline of Scotland remains populated, albeit sparsely and by people who both look and sound different from their predecessors. The Gaelic language continues, as does the Scots, and fine poems written in each are to be found within this collection. The memory of Norse and Irish incursion remains as fresh as ever, although the modern invader is more likely to wield a Hasselblad than a battle-axe. There is still coastal transport and it still rains. Oh, how it rains. Small wonder there is such a longstanding tradition of poetry inspired by water, or with important water references, in Scottish literature.

Like so much from those earlier, stateless times it comes to us through the Gaels. 'Praise of pure water is common in Gaelic poetry,' writes W. J. Watson in his *Bardachd Ghaildheag*, himself quoted by Hugh MacDiarmid at the beginning of his 1937 poem 'The Glass Of Pure Water'. Thus was water poetry squarely established in the Scottish Renaissance, translating across all three indigenous languages, Gaelic, Scots and English. So also was a tremendous breadth of metaphor raised and, MacDiarmid followers might claim, sanctioned.

Although this poem was by no means MacDiarmid's first dip into the water it was the first in which Scots outlook and sensibility met Gaelic subject matter and expressed itself in Scottish English. In 1932 he had written 'Water Music' and, earlier still, in 1925, 'The Watergaw'; this latter being an important part of the vivid and much praised lyrical outpouring in literary Scots that marked his early career. A watergaw, according to the *Concise Scots Dictionary*, is 'an imperfect or fragmentary rainbow' and therefore, I would suggest, the perfect metaphor not only for this collection, but also for the tradition from which it arises. Imperfect, or incomplete; as it must be while still living. Fragmentary; because individualism is so vital to the whole, and I would argue that this is paradoxically true in a country where the ultimate comparator of value and worth rests as much with the community as with the individual.

After the Watergaw may be looked on, therefore, as water poetry following MacDiarmid's; or, since some contributors might refute a positive heritage from this, now historical, figure as a chasing after the unattainable, further additions to the uncompleteable.

Some things do not change because they cannot. Scottish traditions, Scottish culture, are what the physical and emotional landscape makes of them – and what they make of it – growing out of it just as naturally as James Hawkins' *Scots Pine* on the cover of this volume. This is an important point, worthy of note, because it is not wholly true of the people themselves. Earlier peoples were a concoction of Celtic and Norse strains with, eventually, other Britannic intrusions. Almost 300 years of British State and Empire have ensured a still more varied mixing so that future Scots will not look as we look, or as most of us look, just as we do not look like those earlier ones.

Now, of course, there have been substantial influxes from the Indian sub-continent, from Africa and the Caribbean. Men and women who came to work as, say, bus conductors have grandchildren who practice as surgeons or lawyers, and who speak with Scottish accents. It is reasonable to suppose that future generations of Scots will have darker skins and that assumptions inherent in a Pagan/Christian heritage will be moderated by other religions and outlooks.

This does not matter essentially, although I personally look forward to the establishment of the Zen Presbyterian Church Of Scotland. The inhabitants of this country have always been a sturdy, mongrel bunch. They had to be – to survive all that rain. What is truly essential will always win through, and the process of transformation is essential.

Water is ubiquitous in Scotland, as it must be in a mountainous land beside an ocean. It transforms not only in physical terms, by means of irrigation and erosion, but also in spiritual terms, by the uplifting effect of the light that plays on its surface or diffuses through its mass, or by the spirit crushing effect of relentless, never ending downpour. Stand on the summit of Foinavon, in West Sutherland, as the sun sets, and see the thousands of tiny lochans to the north and west shine like scattered coin. Pitch your tent on the machair of any Hebridean island and look out in the morning, watch the ocean's texture change from black velvet through to green, feel its depth. As water is to land, as light is to water, poetry is to language. So the circle closes.

There follows a collection of new poems from Scotland, all broadly inspired by water and beginning, as it must, with compassion. Janet Paisley's *Reading The Bones* gazes across the continents and the sexes to speak for all of us who have ever tried to understand what is far outwith our own experience, brilliantly mimicking her subject's painful gait with her poem's staggered verse structure.

Thereafter the poems are ordered by title with a polite nod in the direction of the alphabet, but on an any-word-will-do basis. This method may offend the rigorously tidy-minded but, by avoiding categories of subject or poet, introduces a random factor that I hope will allow room for chance associations and surprise encounters. As in life, anticipate the unexpected.

The ubiquity of water has ensured that the collection is exceptionally varied. Love poetry searches across the spectrum from Helen Lamb's assertive pragmatism to Brian McCabe's wistful loneliness. There is myth-making from Bashabi Fraser and Christine de Luca, bustling polemic from Bobby Christie and dazzling word play from Robert Crawford. There are adventures in cognition with Hayden Murphy and Gerry Loose as well as surreal visions from Thom Nairn and Ron Butlin. Journeys are made to South America, Ireland and Africa and the sea is visited often, as are wells; wishing wells, drinking wells, clootie wells. All three of the country's languages are represented and, in two cases, writers in Scots have provided glossaries. Wherever Gaelic has been used it has been given primacy, although the writers have, in every case, appended their own translations in English. The collection concludes, as again it must, in celebration. Sheena Blackhall takes us along a gloriously tempestuous river of ideas and images in a boisterous toast to the source of all life.

It is probably fair to say that the poets who offer their works in this collection are at least as aware of the humanity they hold in common with their subjects and their readers as they are of their Scottishness, so no one, wherever they read or hear these words, should feel excluded. That consciousness was built into our tradition at least as early as Burns and probably earlier. They are every bit as aware as their many predecessors that water, in all its forms, is really just the one water, a concept perhaps best expressed by Colin Will in *Water Works* towards the end of the collection.

A culture that cannot see beyond itself and reach out, as this one does yet again, is nothing. For all that, difference is necessary to the process of transformation. Form matters, in life, in nations, in poetry; if only because the ending of difference and individuality resides with stagnation and death.

Scotland continues, as poetry does, ever changing.

Robert Davidson
Last House,
One Benside,
Isle Of Lewis

Tae be life
and tae gie life
we sing

William Hershaw
from *Journey*

Reading The Bones

This time it is not the child
but the man – racked and saddled
by hot sun. Over broken stone,

alone, he walks. Still upright
though burdened with the weight
that brings down worlds. Each step
is iron hard, small insects

dart in sharper shadows, cracks
open in the earth, and grief
is somewhere else – where water is.

The child he walks with is dead
yet he will not set it down.
Beyond the touch of hands, he
is merciless. Does not look back

to where he stopped last, wet
the child's mouth – a smear of mist,
the almost kiss. Does not look

forward though he goes, a slow
sure stepping towards the grave.
Proud head, straight back, the painful
ribs, stripped sticks of arms, and legs

that walk and walk and walk
and are brought down more surely
by the bones I cannot read;

bones he carries on his back.
Is it son or daughter, love
or hope or is he saddled to
the failure of his fatherhood

– the mouth he could not feed,
the need he could not fill, a life
he could not keep – so deep a grief

it cannot be set down. On
and on into the hungry heat,
sweating flies, and every step
an agony of bone and breath.

And I am trying, blindly
to read those bones – of Man,
walking his dead child home.

Janet Paisley

2

Arabesque

two elements
air and water
interact

each meeting
on the plane
of most resistance

air takes water
lifts it tosses it
like dice

throws it
to a height
of sixty feet

makes clouds
that glide
across the surface

of this water
which in turn
takes air

rides with it
impetuous to move
make waves

to travel forward
impelled upon
the instance

by this air
its movement
in complete control

two elements
balletic in response
they dance

entwine
their several beings
interact

Brian Johnstone

Water Barge

Your voice.
It makes a space I can step into
where there is room for me.
It is a journey which holds me,
like the arms of trees.
They bend, they shift slightly,
with the weight, they rock
a little, to accommodate
the fingertips, pressing space
to mould the shapes of words.
When I heard your voice
I knew it was a boat
I could step into; there was
space for me to stretch
my limbs and words; not sink,
but float, on this slow
and gentle barge.

Morelle Smith

Bagh Phabail A-rithist

Trìlleachan ri oir an rathaid
's an fhaoileag shìorraidh a'seòladh
troimhn àile fhionnar,
beanntan Rois is Chataibh ag èirigh
leis an t-seann uaill,
biorach, soilleir,
cumadail,
mar nach do dh'atharraich an saoghal
ann an trì fichead bliadhna,
trì mìle bliadhna 's dòcha
mas ann air muir a laigheas an t-sùil.
Saoil
a bheil Eilean Phabail fhathast am beachd
gu bheil e cumail dìon air a' bhàgh,
no an canadh e ris fhèin
"Shìorraidh, chunna mi bàt'
'na laigh' air a'ghainmhich ghil
is faoileag 'na seasamh air tobht';
nach ann oirnn a thàinig an dà là".

Ruaraidh MacThòmais

Bayble Bay Again

A plover by the roadside
and the eternal seagull coasting
through the cool sky,
the mountains of Ross-shire and Sutherland rise
in their ancient pride,
sharp, clear,
shapely,
as though the world had not changed
in three score years,
three thousand years perhaps
if it is the sea we look at.

I wonder
if Bayble Island still thinks
it guards the bay,
or does it say to itself
"Good heavens, I saw a boat
lying on the white sand
with a seagull standing on a thwart;
how times have changed."

Derick Thomson

The Blessing

Water, great
wherever found,
well, river,
tide-race, fall,
roar, call of
deep to deep
or still pool
lapped by sheep
with dragonflies
in wet meadows
of a soaking spring
without you
many worlds
roll and roll
never green
blue unseen
grit clinker
without you
homes of death
unheard even
a sigh for waves
far less our
floods, our loved
thundering of
great waters.

Edwin Morgan

Water Boy

In fifties Donegal Aunt Kathleen
Didn't have the water in
A good thing too she said
Because the spring was pure and good

And I was the very boy
To fetch that bounty
Clanking two enamelled pails
Down the hawthorned lane
To where beneath the hedge
The water tumbled into a little pool
Of stones polished like jewels
A place of buttercups and celandines

Then the long lug up the hill
The pails heavy as boulders
Pulling my arms knocking my knees
Until I staggered into the dark kitchen
And dumped them onto the stone floor

The water slopped and brimmed the buckets
Like rocking cradles – until it rested –
Twin pools of the necessary and the possible
In that day's domestic economy

Geddes Thomson

Camas

Harry throws fire at midnight
on the green
and we are drawn from sleep
into an ancient dream of midsummer

the dark sea moves ceaselessly
its ebb and flow
is the ebb and flow of my blood
and is constant

far out in the bay under the moon
the *splish splish* of the paddle
is the sound of a sea creature
coming home

leaning against the stone walls of the house
in the time between
which is not day but is light
and is night but is not dark
we are bonded by our silence
silver threads of stillness weave us
into bright patterns of stars
shining on rocks and water
and shadows on the hill
and peace laps our souls

on the high cliff
our feet springing off heather and root
looking out over the sea
higher than the wheeling gulls
we are like gods
we might fly

under the rafters
in the glow of candlelight
we break bread
and share the word

to live is this

Kathy Galloway

9

The Catch

By the Bogie watter
Bee bee boo boo baba
By the Bogie Watter
Bee bee boo boo babala

A cat hunkit on a tree stump
Hissin by the watter
Afore it taks a runnin jump
An sweems awa, a saumon

A horsie wi a mannie
Clip-cloppin by the watter
Till frichtit by a flyin fish
It shrinks, rins aff, a moosie

Then, fit aboot the mannie
Unseated by the watter –
Ach, he's jist a bairnie
I'll pit him in a push-chair

Aff then wi ma mannie
A snochterin eeseless cratur
Thank ye, Bogie watter
I've fulfilled ma weemun's nature

Maureen Sangster

A Sea Change

We move in our new element
swim without learning how
change and are changed
as you, the waters of my flesh
rising to enfold you
rise too, rise in me
plunder the deep that will drag us
under the bed's rocking ocean
our sealed coracle plunging
becomes dolphin, fish, anemone
darker and deeper and down
vast sea roaring round us
to a bed we can never reach
since we must lift again, surface,
fish into dolphin, dolphin into skiff
skimming the water
waves parting, waters into flesh
cold air can touch, toss ashore
on a dry beach, a different coast.

Skin salted by sea's birthing
we lie revealed.
Eyes opened, sunlight dazzled
tide ebbing wordless away.

Moira Forsyth

The Civilising Rain

So you have a HANG-OVER
sorry I will whisper these words –
so you have a hang-over.

Go and take a long drink
from the tap marked COLD.
The water will kill your thirst.

It is that easy this side
of good old comfort planet Earth
as the sweet rain of spring falls

but sadly now for the poor
of this grand old nation of ours
if you can't afford to pay red letters.

Then it's no fresh water for you kid
so people cry – SAVE OUR WATER!
As the civilising rain falls on deaf ears

while on the southern shores of planet Earth
their world of sand is fucking hard
after centuries of kidnap, rape and murder

by us good old northern types:
our banks of course own them to the hilt.
Slavery as economics is still slavery:

fresh water for all human kind
would be so simple but is so hard
for the good old West to give

true and lasting freedom to the South
by freeing these countries
from the fucking World Bank.

This would be as good a start as any
but you and I know that won't happen
so just for now give some money

for WaterAid's vision
is to act in a civilised way –
if modern civilisation was built

on anything it was the written word –
fresh water and of course the gun!
Let's not be like the WAR LORDS

of the West, let the civilising rain
do its funky stuff for the good
cutting out childhood disease, death.

Stopping the spread of poverty –
fresh water can do these things,
and so much fucking more...

Bobby Christie

Sea-Swimming: Clachtoll

Plunge – a howling howl of howls
speeds up from pierced nerve-endings,
punching lungs until they spew it out.

This – is – a – rank – and – cruel – injustice.

Immersion – in an area so close to pain,
adjacent, too, in disconcerting ways,
to pleasure.

Total arrival in the NOW.

Consciousness becomes a temperature-gauge,
stillness is unthinkable, movement
all there is to beat away the bats.

Slowly a pinprick of future glints,
a glow of body heat, return of history.
It is bearable, we are bearing it, we are alive.

Blood and sea-cold reach an equilibrium,
then once again the world is tepid.

Ian MacDonough

A' Coiseachd Anns An Uisge

A' coiseachd ann an uisg an t-samhraidh
fionnarachd an aghaidh a' bhlàiths
smuid an adhair a' dùsgadh
fáile grinn a' ghiuthais.

A' coiseachd anns an uisg a' sileadh
a' lìonadh nan loch 's nan allt
sruth a ghlanadh na srathan
fras a thogadh an spiorad.

A' coiseachd anns an uisge shearbh
a' falamhadh loch 's abhainn
pòg bhàsmhor eile bho dheas
a' grod nan craobh 's nan gleann.

A' coiseachd am brón na h-Ucràine
a' seachnadh nan dileagan meallta
gach h-aon na sgriach péin
a tha fhathast ri chluinntinn.

A' coiseachd an taigh brisg na glainne
a glacadh gathan geura na grèine
talamh tioram teth a' guidhe
air an uisge mharbh.

Walking In The Rain

Walking in the summer rain
coolness defeating warmth
mist of the air wakening
the fine scent of pine.

Walking in the falling rain
filling the lochs and burns
stream that cleansed the straths
shower that lifted the spirit.

Walking in the bitter rain
emptying loch and river
another fatal southern kiss
rotting the trees and glens.

Walking in the sadness of Ukraine
avoiding the deceitful drops
each one a screech of pain
yet to be heard.

Walking in the fragile greenhouse
catching the sun's sharp rays
the dry hot earth praying for
the dead rain.

Peadar Morgan

Dark Side Of The Moon

What with the noisy boys
a mile down the loch
shouting and playing Dark Side of the Moon
of all things
on this sunny day,

that, and this black dragonfly
settled on my book,
I could neither concentrate
nor turn the page.

After I'd seen the silver wings,
black-dashed at the outer edge,
the beaded head and black-furred body
and the tear at the base of a wing,

after I'd heard Pink Floyd
and that "He's no' goat his fucking float wet yet!"

I had to look around,
beyond the cow-churned mud
to pine green hillsides
and birch trees a tree-length away.

A bird rose up
dusty peach as a Barbary dove
but without the clap of wings.
A head, too pointed,
hid among the leaves.

The moment sharpened.

Another, wings tipped white
and barred with blue, flew up.

A third pottered briefly in a tuft
and a fourth confirmed them jays,
looping up the lochside
from bush to tree to shade,
shy and quiet and as rare
as the dark side of the moon.

Valerie Thornton

Deòir

Dreug, dreug, dreug
tha mo thap a'deuradh uisge

dreaghaidh mo chùinnseas mi
'stionnaidh mi dhe e

a'smaoaineachadh air na teangean tiachuinnt ud
ann an dùthchannan ceine

Dia thoir maitheanas dhuinn uile
's mi smocadh mo mhile cigarrette.

Tears

Drip, drip, drip
my tap drips water like tears

my conscience pricks me
and I turn it off

thinking of those parched tongues
in these distant lands

God forgive us all
as I light my thousandth cigarette.

Catriona Montgomery

Dreams, Dumfries And Landscapes
(for Frances Corcoran)

In garden blooms a newflower.
Yellow suns peep at a crimson moon.

For a short life wading in
From a rainbow comes a Red Admiral.

On low tide stranded boats, tipped
On moondunes, sail among cowslips.

A velvet black caterpillar saunters
Out at noon. No flights yet.

A red kite creaks through
To the back room of my window,
A zoo-site tugging at a year's perspective.

Accentless, migrating entomology
Clutching a flight ticket, happily
Stranded on water's wheelbarrow.

Goldfinches, Cranesbill,
Dragonflies, breathing heat
On sunbathing Salvia.

Gate swinging, yellow striped
Hoverflies make up a Plague-Aphid
Parading on a Continental Drift.

On stone, wings turn over
For a moth-tan, white tipped
Wings are paled pleasure with honey.

Colours in nettles are green-vined
Wined edges with white flecks wind-frothed.

Silk grasses are winged, shunning
All but pollen winded lovelights.

Sober peacocks pair for life.
Butterflies in bog-bean have purple hearts.

With lowtide sunsand has beehives,
The garden's fleet is tiding out.

Crimson moon is beaming on yellow suns.
In garden blooms a newflower.

Hayden Murphy

Shaman Of The Elements

A flood fierce enough to sweep a town away,
a sea of tranquillity to float dreams on

you make Earth blue, grass green
and when you tumble from

the pitcher of the sky, the darkness gleams
with a trillion silver arrowheads in flight.

Shaman of the elements –
you freeze the eyelash of the Inuit to white,

you wet the worker in the paddy field,
you caul the mountains with your mist

the beauty of your dew upon a spider's web
or on a quivering leaf

makes poets lift their pens to write.

Shape-shifter – wake me from my dreams
with water which once graced a glacier in Tibet.

Christen the infant at the font with snowflakes
that once melted on the Hudson or the Seine.

Quench my thirst with drops which glistened
on a Pharaoh's brow, or in a brickie's sweat.

Sweet water – ancient salt-tongued sculptor,
whose tides define the edges of our lands,

whose strength has crumbled cliffs to grains of sand,
fall gently on my upturned face,

seduce me with your fingers' pattering dance,
share with me a lover's last embrace.

Water, Wasser, Uisge, Eau and a million unknown names –

Slumbering in a reed-fringed loch, you are
a shining mirror for the universe

shimmering as a rainbow in the sky, you stir
the pagan in my soul –

from deserts and sickbeds the dying call for you,
in a thousand tongues the drowning curse your power.

Show mercy when I'm waving to the shore –
let the boatman row me safely over.

Magi Gibson

The Shallow-Enders

The shallow-enders
sploosh and splash with
their green cork frog floats,
their yellow plasticy body rings,
their giant blue inflatable swans.

The shallow-enders,
as if Jacques Cousteau,
plunge into the shallow depths
from the rubber orange submarine
in water as busy as a Dunkirk beach.

The shallow-enders
breast stroke with
stiff necks and dry hairdos held
high gossiping as they swim
in whatever direction takes their fancy.

The shallow-enders,
with their amateur strokes
carelessly crossing the bows
of fellow flounderers flapping
oblivious to the approaching torpedo

of

The man who is
decked out like an Olympic medalist
and who *has* to achieve his nightly quota of lengths
while doing his butterfly by the proverbial book
taking no prisoners in his foamy froth

as he leaves the flotsam
of beleaguered shallow-enders
bobbing like debris in his wake.

Brian Whittingham

Three Ullapool Epistles

On a beach near Lochinver   *(To Sara Dodd)*

That Hardy-chase we raced through – finding
in his disordered collected works just the poems
our needs remembered, over long-distance phone –
with Hardy alive for us we're never alone.
Yet where is he? Pages turn like seaweed
agitated by strong tide
obscuring shallows and relative deeps
and items for which the seagull swoops.
We are fishers and carrion hunters, our pounce
replicated that seal's which appears to dance
for itself in the bay, but is needful, hungry.
Some irreducible sense of humanity
we quest for, in the shifting currents of books
no deeper, perhaps, than the green sea of the bay.

Seacliffs facing Suilven: why Samuel Becket is funny
(To Bill Dunlop)

Deep sea fishermen won't learn to swim
so the best writers, braced on cliffs
know what they fear, what we all fear.
In pages which only a coward would skim
they tell us we're cowards, what we can't bear
in places where we're not *big* she or him
but always shivering children, distressed by ifs.
Oh, we have tae'en too little care of this –
not what we salvage from the gale's whim
not the quirky pleasure of a parting kiss
but the fisherman's knowledge: when you slip you're gone,
why struggle? You've lost all on which sun shone,
woman, son, daughters, in one big miss,
while cackling beggars survive without bliss, on air.

North shores   *(To Tom Lowenstein)*

We disagree about when we first met –
I think, on a CND march, you, at a Cambridge lecture –
but I know that since then I've never felt out of touch,
as if pigs flew and brothers were brotherly.
Once, turning back inland on Hoy, we met you walking
towards the dock we'd driven to fetch you: uncanny –
the man with a crow in his pocket (as it were)
from the North shore of Alaska, where your books would take us.
We each guessed, at our Queens and Kings Colleges,
that truth was far away, in scanter places,
on tips of rock which sudden sun embraces
where redthroat or Great Northern loons wing
above sea green over sand, blue, otherwise gray
which drenches and buoys up our different samelike knowledges.

Angus Calder

Erosion

He had the best of you.
He broke you but you healed.
The broken parts calcified and became
hardened pebbles in your soft sediment.

I flow across you
with my soft water.
It wears away the sediment
but those pebbles remain.

Only a heavy hammer
or a sharp chisel
would crack them.
I have only soft water.

Peter Whiteley

Fae Eden, A Burn

Fae Eden, a burn raise
an smaa smoor
blissit da breer.
Whaar springs gret
folk gaddered
an newsed,
biggit wells,
an fillt daffiks.
An whaar burns
gaffed ower stanes,
dey wöshed,
guddled fish,
an bairns puddled
i da frush.

Here water
pulses trowe lives,
unsung, unseen.
Lik aa göd things,
lik da well, da spring,
we only miss hit
whin hit's gien,
rins dry.

From Eden, A Stream

From Eden, a stream rose
and a light drizzle
blessed the first shoots.
Around tearful springs
folk gathered
and gossiped,
sunk wells,
and filled buckets.

And where streams
laughed over stones,
they washed, guddled
fish with bare hands,
and children paddled
in the froth.

Here, water
pulses through lives,
unsung, unseen.
Like all good things,
like the well, the spring,
we only miss it
when it's gone,
runs dry.

Christine De Luca

Figurehead

The fog thickens,
I see no ships.
The gulls left days ago

Ebbing into the wake
Like friends grown tired
Of chasing failure.

I miss their uncouth snatch and grab
Their loud insatiable hunger.
I see nothing but fog.

Before my ever open eyes
The horizon has closed in
The world's end dissolved.

I lumber on, grudging my status –
I'm purpose-built to dip and toss
My cleavage, crudely carved

To split waves
My hair caked with salt
My face flaking off.

Dilys Rose

Freshwater Poet
(for Les Murray)

You can sink like a hunter into your own forest
and find medicine in its moss and silences.

Some men could track for days, with arrows dipped
in deadly irony, and never fetch a single poem home

yet words drop to your palm wherever you part the branches,
floating from a to b. There's an alphabet ocean in here,

waves folding over like pages of vast foreign dictionaries
and a species of blue leaf ghost fish that never

thrashed in any angler's net. Forest swimmer,
your lazy breast-stroke could outlast the Flood.

Easy enough, then, to block out the North Sea this morning,
deploying your lack of gravitas against the eastern window

and distilling fresh water from salt so we can taste and see
it isn't sea, and you're not walking on it

just pointing from the shore towards one who can.

James McGonigal

Fuireach Is Fàgail

nuair a sheòl thu a chuain
cha tug thu an cuan leat
no àrneis suarach d'òige, ach an t-eilean,
àluinn gun phris, thubairt thu,
dh'fhoghnadh fionnarachd a thobraichean
's uillt, easan agus lochain, thubairt thu,
mar gun cumadh iadsan
gach tart air falbh

cha b'e siud an t-òran
a lìon na stòpanan
le deòir do leanna, cha b'e
siud an dòchas a chùm thu
thall far an robh na dolairean,
cha b'e siud an sruth briathrach
a chùm do sgòrnan bog

's co dhiù, cha chreideadh tu
na tha san uisge eòlach seo fhathast
de dh'uisgeachan –
burn leugach, poll donn, sàl,
sàl, tìm, fithich air iteag, 's gach
seòrsa deoch slàinte drùidhteach
dhan fheadhainn a dh'fhalbh 's
a tha ri teachd

ach a bhràthair ghràdhaich, inns' dhomh,
bheil am paghadh ort, eil an t-eilean
fhathast mar a bha, nad chuimhne, gleus air
caibe 's capull 's lainntirean, an talamh
ùr, fiarach, an linne sèimh, beò le
sgiathan airgid, gun for air gaise, clach,
no deanntag, eil an t-eilean ('s tu air a chuin)
fhathast mar a bhà (do shùil thar na fàire far
an do phasgadh e sìos), eil thu
deanamh gàire nuair a chuimhnicheas tu
ort fhèin, san am òg fhionnar ud
a sheòl thu
amach tromh na frasan

Staying And Leaving

when you sailed across the ocean
you did not take the ocean with you,
or the miserable furnishings of your childhood,
only the island, beautiful and priceless, you said,
sufficiency in the cool freshness of its springs,
streams, waterfalls and pools, you said,
as if they
could keep every thirst at bay

that wasn't the song
which filled the tankards
with the tears your ale shed, that
wasn't the hope that kept you
there where the dollars were,
that wasn't the eloquent stream
that kept your throat moist

besides, you won't believe
how rich this familiar water remains
in waters –
jewelled spring, peat-brown pool, brine,
brine, time, flight of ravens, and all kinds of
drenching toasts to the health of
those who have gone, and those
who are to come

but, beloved brother, tell me,
are you thirsty, is the island
still as it was, in your memory, the sheen of use
on every spade, horse, lantern, the earth
fresh, grassy, the fish-pool still, alive with
silver wings, no thought for withering, for stone
or nettle, does the island (while you're still at sea)
remain as it was (your eye beyond the horizon where
it had folded away), do you remember
how you were, in that cool young time
when you sailed
out through the showers

Aonghas MacNeacail

Fush Legend

Three mountains cam dunnerin oot o the west,
Ilk yin wi a burn flingit ower its shouther,
An aye as they gaed an aye when they stude
The wecht o them champit the grun tae a pouther.

An yin eftir ither they cast tae the ocean
Their burn like a bricht pirlin raip on a rod;
An saumon an troot cam skimmerin oot
As if they were lowpin up ladders tae God.

The mountains were spreckelt wi lochans lik pooches,
Fashioned o peat an weill theekit wi reeds;
An intae them fushes bi thoosans gaed skinklin
Doun amang daurkness an cauldness an weeds.

Syne when thae three wis aw stappit fou,
Wi the burns on their backs an the sun in their een,
They trauchelt awa tae the edge o the warld,
Boolders an stanes markin whaur they had been;

An hunkerin doun wi their heids in the cloods,
An on each shank a lang white wreath for a hushion,
They hae faan intae dreams o troot in their pooches
An saumon, frae when they gaed east for the fushin.

James Robertson

Water

Water
Drown
Fountain of life
Love floating on water
Antenatal dream of amniotic water
Dripping with life
Water in blood
                    water on the brain
                                    watery fantasies
Of ecstatic sinking into bubbling ocean
Purple fish
            coral
                    red spikes
                            painful beauty
Irrigate the land
Blast with stormy rain
Drink in the desert
Elixir of life
Crystal clear and sparkling
Pristine pure
Transparent translucent
Invisible rainbow-coloured
Water

Tim Cloudsley

Southern Geometries

The first month is mountain light above a river flat
a boathouse   the bleached-out boards of a jetty
rowboats on a lake green yellow blue   and swimmers
whose arms are thrown back calling to one another
and to those who shake chequered picnic cloths or
dangle brown legged babies into the hardly rippling water
in the still Glenorchy morning   Here they are:
their colours blots of washing on the line of the retina
flattened for a split second   into delightful lozenges
of lapis lazuli   pink trapezoids   vermilion
arabesques across the fluctuating field of vision
the vee of reflection that tips them into its opposite
its split diamond twin   across which
like brilliant telescopic fish   minute climbers
are obliquely linked along a fiery splint of frozen light
their attitudes fixed for the shutter's blink
the flat silver triangles vee'd into ice   shades raised
to a sunburst beyond the gullies' steep blue angles
or tilted to reflect sheer turquoise   a skewed polygon
across which minute swimmers are dots suspended
across a graph in the briefest moment of deep January
before all the geometries again go whirling
(ascending and descending) on diagonals of refraction.

Gerrie Fellows

Water Dream Ghost

...the smoky smirr o rain...

George Campbell Hay

Grey-white haar over the dew-furred hummocks
between which standing water, and below
the rain-fed plenty of the table,

you will lift, benign ghost of vapour,
and these dark weeds and grasses dry,
final droplets of your smile glint at the sun.

On morning air and moisture your smile persists,
over unwalked nowheres gulls and herons pace
or find concealment in, no man's marshland.

Above you towers this town built up with funds
demolished built again and built again
when it was dark with iron industry
and coal hauled out from tunnels water fills
these years since all this ended, and the sky
(now bleak with building and the steelworks' going)
burst orange whiles from furnace iron, steel...

Somewhere ghost dreams of sodden moss arise,
and pools, and drinking water, and the child
rolling and laughing light mawkit with glaur.

Dry and cracked, old pages, sad old men
and sprouted crops beyond harvesting,
if your grandsons lack the life of childish play

grandfathers have still where this ghost appears –
the ghost's long glint in those bright laughter-tears –
may parched earth yet well strong and slake their drouth.

Robert R. Calder

The Gift Of Water

*(From a combination of Celtic and other myths, where a girl sits impris-
oned. Her tears create a stream and her sighs, the wind. One day she
realises that she needs to will her own freedom, and once she is free, the
stream of her tears becomes the life-giving gift of water, as the girl – the
symbol of fertility – is wed to the sun.)*

There is a beautiful girl in a cave
Where I can hear her weep
Singing sad tunes that ripple the wave
As she sings herself to sleep.

She weeps for her land
She weeps for her love
She weeps to be free and run
She looks for a hand
To stretch from above
And open her cave to the sun.

The wave runs into wave to set
The youthful stream aflow
Which has been born of tears spent
In darkness and in woe.

'Till one day she turns around to face
The awning so long barred
And climbs the rock to greet the space
Where her stream flows undeterred.

The stream now gathers grace and strength
To widen bank and bed
To create springs and lochs of length
In lonely glens, that know instead
Of tears, they now can bring
The gift of water from her being –
Free to live and free to love
And free to wed the sun above.

Bashabi Fraser

Horseshoe Crab In Flagrante Delicto

Full moon and a grey piece of the moon
slips out of the restlessness, the sea.
Say a million years, say four hundred,
and begin with her again:
life is lisping in the water,
the Earth is just rising.

As usual, she's lugging her man,
gaining the globby sand.

She'll let him do what she likes,
bury it, and get back.

An abstract spider,
she'll re-enter the fusses of the foam,
see the glint in the deep
and head for that struggling moon,
the moon in the ocean's web,
the moon's mime and its warning.

Richard Price

Paean To The Hydrosphere
(extracted from a work in progress)

Forced through hot geysers as a jet of steam,
rolled down scoured canyons in a rapid river,
traced to a high source up an unsure stream,
close to where the melt line lies and into mire,
held in taps and standpipes for a million towns,
channelled to strong slipstream over massive weir,
locked in ice-caps and the saline oceans,
filtered through soil, through rock, through air –

tapped by deep borehole to its lowest table,
raised from mud ditches in buckets hung on wheels,
banked back on terraced hillsides, left to trickle,
lapped on vast flooded flats of paddy fields,
scooped from still ground tank with pivoted beam ladle,
bound up by laden thunderheads in columned piles,
strapped between civic pool-walls lined with polished tiles,
and everywhere it travels, fickle, stable,

        this liquid entity contained
            yet constantly unstill,
        this infinite limpidity,
           this bob, this swill,
        this massive ball in gravity
           of readily-must-spill
        ocean that slaps the belly
           of the world's great barrel
               in its tidal straps and ties
               that warmth kittles into skies
                  where aquarian suspension
                     on carrier winds that bear
                     a humid burden heavier
                     than their own weight in air
                  distributes its light dancers everywhere
                     over land and ice and ocean,
                  moisture that climbs mountains like a stair
                  and is perpetually in motion –

Colin Donati

A Week On The Island
(for Michael Gassenmeier)

On the first morning, he did not
See even one. On the second, he noticed,
Out of the corner of his eye, a shining
Disappearing beneath the surface of the sea.

On the third, he watched a wet head,
Rising. On the fourth, he stole a kipper
From the breakfast table and carried it, wrapped
In the morning newspaper, down to the beach.
He threw it, head first, into the sea.

On the fifth, he saw a seal, hauled out
On a rock. He took another kipper and walked
Along the coast, with it in his hand. The seal swam
In closer. On the sixth, he was given a kipper
By the waitress and, with the rest of the hotel
Guests watching, took it to the waiting seal.

On the seventh, the seal came right up
To him, and almost took the fish straight
From his hand. He walked back, up the pebbled
Beach, to the hotel, and started to pack.
He steadied himself for the homeward flight,
And for his other life, so many miles inland.

Gordon Meade

I Trace Your Name

                    in sand before
the water's edge; whether the spell
will take, I cannot tell
                 the tide
being neither out nor in
clear direction hard to fathom

the dark sand wet and firm
my finger drawing sure resistance
sand-flies, shells, a small stone
dark and smooth:

                I cannot read
you at this distance, cannot waive
the sand
        stray letters swirling
tidal waters

Anne MacLeod

Journey

We were taen up
out the dinnlin roar
o saut sea sang.
Rising, we were wrocht
in sillar cloud – womb
cairried miles ower tummlin ocean
tae fa saftly out the West,
brithirs and sisters,
abune the Lomond Hills.

Tae be life
and tae gie life,
we sing.

Now we meet up aince mair
on leaf, stem, stane an blade
And jine as ane.
A cleir bricht eel
threids atween root an rock,
mells as puddle, pool and burn.
Hamewirth.
Aye hame an doonwirth,
aye doon we pour
intil trout-lair an loch,
flood land for grey goose and wing-beat.
A tod laps neir.

Tae be life
and tae gie life,
we sing.

We are jewels,
no ane o us less precious
than the ithirs,
ma brithirs and sisters.
Whit hae we been and whit will we be?

Bluid that beats,
snawflake and haar hardened tae ice,
malt fae the grains we lousen fae the barley,
the tear that fae the een doonfa's
wi lauchter or wae.
We baptise the man-bairn,
we slocken the drouth in the thirsty thrapple,
we fa on the hot earth,
we skail and slosh in time's reservoir.

Tae be life
and tae gie life,
we sing.

And now we heid doon the Cut and hear,
faur aff, the thrummlin saut sea sang again.
We gae back, we gae back,
And though adventures divert and dam us
we never resist
and nae force resists us.
We gae back tae jine in the mither pool.
They file us, transform
but we never stap,
restless, ettlin, aye movin,
driven bi gravity, wind and tide,
the ingines that wheel the world.
Ower the girn o the tractor,
the hirsel o the fields we hear
the saut sea sang that surrounds
the island continents.

Tae be life
and tae gie life,
we sing.

We rub oot the reid stain
and fa through the fingers
o the frantic queen.

We rin ower the taes o the foolish king.
We skail out the basin o the governor
for nae Pilate maun haud us up.

A sang, a formless poem,
a liquid chorus
o endless rhymes,
tae be life
and tae gie life,
we sing.
We were taen up
out the dinnlin roar
o saut sea sang.

William Hershaw

Note: The poem follows the journey of a rain drop from its making in a cloud over the Atlantic Ocean until it falls above the Lomond Hills and runs into Loch Leven. From there it flows through a man made waterway, known as 'The Cut', on its passage to the North Sea.

Glossary: *dinnlin:* deafening; *saut:* salt; *wrocht:* fashioned, made; *siller:* silver; *fa:* fall; *abune:* above; *tod:* fox; *louse:* loosen; *slocken:* slacken; *drouth:* thirst; *thrapple:* throat; *skail:* spill; *thrummlin:* trembling; *fyle:* dirt; *ettlin:* trying; *girn:* complaining cry; *hirsel:* rustle; *taes:* toes; *maun:* may; *haud:* hold.

44

Water Lesson

Puddle-gazing at
the school gate, the wee girl minds
on the day's homework.

"Bring something to make
the class think deeply of our
water-barren lands."

Reaching down to catch
a rainbow's reflection, she'll
bring fresh tears instead.

Liz Niven

Like Ophelia

It was the time you were pushed in the burn.
You were twelve, you were drunk.
Ropes of hair floated
on and off cheekbones
wet under November moons
on helicopter rotors.
Rainbow fountain;
a Technicolor raft of vomit
floods through moonbeams and foam.
The legs! Nothing.
The legs! Nothing.
The arms! Still but undulating.
Fingers pierce the water's miniscus
into the cold slabs of night,
troughing and stabbing
sine waves in air.

Your ears sunk
into claustrophobic pleasures of water,
surfaced and surfaced and sunk
into the chill
of being young
and drunk;
afraid of staying;
of going home;
or not going home.
Paralytic.

Rise white Skinners with green moss.
Rise slime filled holes in your Doc's.
Rise Wrangler jacket of dark blue lead.
Rise Simon shirt soaked to your skin.

Tubes of breath suck.
Mad moons spinning.
Sick—sick—sick.
Oh hail Mary full of grace...
God remove me from this mess...
now and at the hour...
That was it – move or your dead.
Death – alone in the Burn. The burn
and the night sucking you into stars.

But fuck it you were going to stand.
To roll over and your head sunk
like a cat compress up through
the glossy hiss of surface.

How did you ever stand up?
Stagger home on liquid legs.
People staring and saying your name
and stepping aside into numb echoes.
You made it through alleys and blackouts.
To your father's familiar fists.

How did you ever stand up from
cold funeral water?
Child in burn drowning with
grasses of forget-me-nots.
Empty fag packets of poppies.
A virginity of pansies.
A naive dream of daises.
Purple waterfalls of violets.
Yourself a fucked up rose.
Like Ophelia you were mostly under water.
You let innocence drown
and went home neither man nor boy.
Unlike Ophelia you would never be pushed down again.

Des Dillon

Loch Ard

Glistened with fresh-loch water as I lay
down on the bank, my dog beside me shook
clear droplets from his fur, the curtained spray
rainbowing sunshine. Fixed in close-eyed look,

the swan whose habitat our swim invaded,
neck-questing, paddled towards our grassy shore,
then flapped a breadth of wings and, head down, waded
across the shingle, till its running bore

down on us with an outraged angry screech
croaking through wings that on ungainly feet
flapped menace to avenge the lapping breach
our wake rolled through its rushes of retreat.

I jumped up, grabbing hasty clothes and towel,
and fled the bare assertion of its claim;
after a nervous mandatory growl
my dog, through backward glances, did the same.

The swan turned round, the waddled water's edge
re-floating ruffled whiteness that propelled
it back to its mate, half-hidden under sedge,
nesting the future, mottled and unshelled.

Maurice Lindsay

Love On The Braes

We sighed over the white sea
after we'd climbed the brae
above the Sound of Sleat.
The shimmer was a shiver
for earthbound creatures grown far
from the watery womb of life.

Reassuringly, the isles were there:
bold shapes abreast the tides
and the phallic Cuillin thrust.
Autumn slopes spilled, loch on loch,
silver-splattered under the randy sun.

A stag roared and roared and
with his harem circled our cairn
oblivious of all but lust.
Symbolic waters urged. We swam;
after, in the browning bracken,
by dewy starlight, soft as sphagnum,
found our peace.

Hamish Brown

Africa, Man

Being Africa,
you can make the excitement meter
go real high.
Like you know, man,
you're in this really wild place.
You can have a lot of fun.

The Smoke That Thunders
tolerates bungee jumpers
surfers and white water rafters.

In the town of Vic Falls itself
you can see this really neat craft village.
It's not as tacky as you might think.
You can learn things here
that you would probably only find in the guide book.

For every ten pounds you spend
one pound goes to
local community schools
like the one here.

At night you can eat
the animals you've seen
during the day.

Tourism can really help
to save the planet.

Tusk tours
two weeks
2,245 pounds.

Elephants, nose to tail, passing
dust rising from the orange soil
unmarked paths crossing
tourist tracks
fluorescent green and yellow and pink
anoraks gathering to gawp
and snap photos before the animals
disappear and to prove that
we were here.

Words can't describe
Victoria Falls decked out in
fashion conscious Livingstones
and white rhino
precious only because
they are the last of their kind
a rare commodity in their rarity.

Been there
done it
got the tee-shirt.
*Africa, man
what a trip.*

Dan R. Skinner

Blind Man By The River

For fifty years he has touched base here,
stepping through the valley he knows perfectly,
tree by oak-trunk or root-railing,
topsoil waterlogged under the grass,
autumn drakes fighting and flailing
as the leaf-bringing gale subsides.

He knows exactly what it is like.
The sounds tie in with his pictures.
The river, rising and falling like his own life,
whispers its metric philosophy,
swishing round the fox-trails into the dog-roses,
instantly sensitive to rainfall in the hills.

He blends with the varied pathways along the banks,
moves in their half-shade, disperses mists.
He tastes the articulate water on his fingertips.
He blinks, and the water is sharp black and white.
Pausing at the seat, facing down-river,
the cuckoo gone, he hears the woodpecker.

Having lost his sight but not his vision
he dreams through time, translating the riverside
into its paraphrased reworded epic,
ever-running, actors and extras squirrelling
and gliding, a confluence long ago begun
of gleaming stanzas set to the evening sun.

Sally Evans

Saddens Me

now to remember us in bed together
rolling and tumbling till finally
dawn eased that day through the window
and later – after croissants and coffee –
we were back upstairs to wash
away all trace of each other.

What fools we were
(scrubbed to the cleanest of breaks)
and now whenever I hear the
gurgling goodbye of bath water
it seems to echo and swell
until I fear I might drown
in this   in this the distance
between   us.

No one understands a man
who loves his bed bugs.

Pete Fortune

Meander

on Kelvin banks
turn of currents
on land in water

feeling the bend

feeling the flow

Alistair Paterson

The Tay Moses

What can I fashion
for you but a woven
creel of river –
rashes, a golden
oriole's nest, my gift
wrought from the Firth –

and choose my tide; either
the flow, when water-tight,
you'll drift to the uplands –
my favourite hills; held
safe in eddies, where salmon,
wisdom and guts
withered in spawn,
rest between moves: that
slither of body as you were born;

or the ebb, when the water
will birl you to snag
on reeds, the river –
pilot leaning over the side:
"Name o God!" and you'll change hands
tractor-man, grieve,
to the farm-wife, who
takes you into her competent arms

even as I drive, slamming
the car's gears;
spitting gravel on tracks
down between berry fields,
engine still racing, the door wide,
as I run toward her, crying
LEAVE HIM! *Please,*
it's okay, he's mine.

Kathleen Jamie

River Ness
after drawings by David Connearn

1. upriver

does the *Garry Dog,*
holding a yellowhair course,
in the swollen fall
give way to
Jock Scott
Thunder and Lightning
Stoat's Tail?
bristling in
the brackish rise

2. seaward

bottlenose at Munlochy buoy
discount the deeper route to North
holding for the safer slack
call it a couple of hours at springs
pilot pick-up at the Meikle Mee
petroleum bulk, Polish coal, Baltic wood
leaving the Runac hard
two second starboard hand
well to green

Ian Stephen

1. names of classic salmon flies
2. navigation marks for approaching Inverness harbour

Oceans Of Childhood

my house holds tight
as the tides of my children
surge   in   and   out

swamping
   then stranding me
among tiny bits of paper
cut   up   on   the   floor
cold cups of tea
dirty clothes
cascading
     down
        the
           stairs
whorls of dog hair
wafting   in the door draft

my house breathes
   hello   and   goodbye
   come back   stay away

to babies metamorphosing
into unknowable adults
faintly familiar
in their laughter and eating habits

all this
flowing in and out
routine and random
   my house sighs and sings

and soaks the erratic ebb and flow
the fluidity of childhood

while visiting currents
   swirl warmly around us
leaving salt water memories
like white dust

Cynthia Rogerson

Off The Map

We abandon the map
head into the cleft between
two soft breasted hills.

The burn gives a line to follow
a backwards path against the flow.

You want to know where we are
– exactly.

I say – here.

When we look back
the road has disappeared
and there is shining water.

Around the bend, another
fall, another fall
until –

We come to a pool
blacker than imagination
deeper than you or I dare go.

We paddle round the edges
play games with our reflections.
You say you know me.

You and your definitions.
I kick cold water over you.
Love isn't logical. It's just true.

Helen Lamb

Mrs Oliphant Drifts Shorewards
(extracted from Impossibility)

Under the North Sea, a mile off Elie
Where once she was noticed in a mullioned window
White lace cap rising, brooding over her table,
Margaret Oliphant Wilson Oliphant
Translates on to starfish and nacred shells
Montalembert's *Monks of the West*

Still weary, awash with hackwork to support
Dead Maggie, Marjorie, Tiddy, and Cecco,
Her water babies, breathing ectoplasm,
She watches aqualungs glow with shellac,
Mindful how she loves light's aftermath,
Protozoa's luminescent wash

On the Firth of Forth; she drifts
Eagerly shorewards, can almost touch
Piers at St Andrews, cybery, Chopinesque fingers
Of Tentsmuir Sands, Blackwood's Strathtyrum
Pressure-resistant, bathyscaphic den
Deeply upholstered with morocco books

Ich bien Margaret Oliphant
Je suis Margaret Oliphant
I am Margaret Oliphant
You are Margaret Oliphant
Vous etes Margaret Oliphant
Sie sind Margaret Oliphant

I love my home, its *lares et penates*
Of broken shoe buckles, balls of green wool,
Needles, its improvisatory architecture
Feeding my work with interruptions, turns
Snatched, forty-winked; stashed seed pearls in a dish
Radiate homely incarnational light

Sometimes the green walls glimmer, elverish,
Phosphorescent, spectrally alive,
Razorfish splay galvanised medium's fingers
Seeking burnished heads of polyps and corageen
Brocaded with plankton, nuzzled by antlered snails,
Vulval, brasslit, flecked and veined and washed

Dinner-suited Auchterlonian clubmen
Fill the fishtank windows of the R & A;
Subsea, in my dark, Victorian
Antimacassered, embroidered sewing room,
I'm inky, threaded with spectra, gynaecological
Eyeball thistle-tassels of the sea

Brown, blue-grey, single-cell-like
Pre-embryo materials in store
But never used, spermatozoic spirits
Haunt the sunned waters, seances of plankton lie
Paperweight-still, flower heads, floating marbles
Undulating in slow liquid glass

I am too antisyzygously Scottish,
Thirled to names like Eden, Wallyford,
Pittenweem; tidally to and fro
Mights and maybes captivate me, I waver
Between hot toddy and hard, cold-boiled chuckies
Smooth and rounded as a baby's skull

Oceans teem with informational currents;
Lord Kelvin's submarine telegraphy
Nets continents; minke whales, prawns,
Mackerel and reef-life hover, agog
Though bored by its contents: same old same old
Verisimilitudinous whine

When Alexander Diving Bell invented the xenophone
I heard his voice calling, "The sea! The sea!"
Hollowly into a shell
As if he could contact Robert Louis Verne
Or all the impossible, massed, forlorn spirits
Edinburgh exiled, waving from twenty thousand leagues

Robert Crawford

1½

St Triduana's Well and Chapel, Restalrig:
among the graveyard's still apparent skull-and-crossbones
there's a sign, that the chapel keys can be collected
at DECORUM, Painting and Decorating Contractors,
9–5 Weekdays. Somebody's taken the trouble
to mark nearby: PINK FLOYD, NIRVANA, BEAST McPHILLIPS.

The unusual hexagonal chapel was built for James III
above a spring, and the floor-slabs, laid below ground level,
would have been underwater: became, much later, linked
with Triduana, an "obscure Pictish saint",
who gifted a princely suitor enamoured of her eyes
those eyes on thorns; was granted her desired seclusion.

The waters, like her intercession, the blind's remeid;
all mere idolatrie, in the Reformers' eyes,
who tumbled down the upper part: the lower, since
restored, re-roofed, kept dry with pumps, is bare except for
a wooden figure rising above the streams of sunlight,
plotting a king's descent into humility.

High up on the outside wall, somebody's taken the trouble
to record, twice, with a permanent marker, the name: SHEREE.
The enormous trees are beginning their meditations on autumn,
and beyond the ordered, secular windows of
the Pensions Department, in which so much has been invested,
the golden-antlered flanks of Holyrood unfold.

Where a well-house stands, the chapel's
miniature double, exact
down to the floral bosses,
but pumpless: mosses thrive,
and a pipe dribbles water
into a pool of water.

A small-mesh grill bars
the aperture, bars touch,
taste, the chance to test it,
but wishes are still admitted;
coins, their remnants, dot
the flooded chamber's floor.

Ken Cockburn

Rain Maker's Paint Box

i. Black (poison)

Troubled water silts my dreaming
choking my song with viral stink.

ii. Red (drought)

Sunset streams, rich blood
of Highland Rainmaker (who opens his veins
in wild transfusion, paints *our* desert
with a monsoon brush)

iii. Gold (slake)

Gold trout slash a mountain pool –
jealous marsh marigolds
polish their own burnished brass.

iv. Silver (quench)

I saw a shoal of mackerel
explode argent angels
from a sea-wrack prison.

v. Green (snowmelt)

Pilgrims, cool your lesions
in our healing wells.

Pure fluxions on your blistered tongues.

Soothe your feet
in our dripping grass.

Quench, and bide.

Tom Bryan

The Passenger

I came to the banks of Lethe
and approached the ferryman:
I asked how much he charged
for a single, no return.

I looked across the river
as it rippled in the breeze
then stepped into the rowing-boat
as he took up the oars.

Your fare, he said, for crossing
in this weather, on this night
is your last drawn breath
and your last eye-light.

Will you take a poem instead:
I have one in my throat?
But it swelled there choking
with wads of paper notes.

My blood it is the stream
my breath it is the wind
my body forms the boat
for the ferryman: my mind.

Tessa Ransford

One World Plughole

```
                H
        E               E
M                               M
I                               I
        S               S
                P
        H               H
E                               E
R                               R
        E               E
                S
```

Colin Dunning

Poaching Salmon

Many's the night
I have used dusk for a wrap
And slipped my image into a world
Where soft voices stole out of shadows,
Rippling through the air like an owl's call,
And made more eloquent by the
Music of rustling leaves.

Salmon, in a velvet-deep pool,
Reared up out of the water,
Bright, silvery flutes, startling
The coming dark with their melodies;
Orchard trees came alive in the wind,
Weaving and singing,
Their wombs ripe, rich and full,
Pregnant with apples;
And the ungrieving river,
Lurid in the moon's sheen,
Eased out of her dark labyrinths
In a serpentine dance of the dispossessed
As enmeshed fish began their slow
Dance with death.

Sam Gilliland

A Prayer Journey For Water

Child across her hip, gourd upon her head,
she looks for small streams – does not know rivers.
Bless the dry wayfaring of the thirst led.

Her eyes are fixed on the desert ahead.
Swaying as she walks, her long hands hold her
child across her hip, gourd upon her head.

She knows her needs; to cook and make bread,
sweet water for her children to savour.
Bless the dry wayfaring of the thirst led.

How long can she seek? Her legs are as lead.
She must go on, must stop, go on with her
child across her hip, gourd upon her head.

Neither words, nor songs, nor faith but instead
many pregnancies and patient labours.
Bless the dry wayfaring of the thirst led.

Shading her child's face she gives him her breast,
all things that go out are also prayers.
Child across her hip, gourd upon her head,
bless the dry wayfaring of the thirst led.

Robert Davidson

Precious

Log cabin alive with small children
and a scarcity of water.
I remember two large pails
and how far I had to carry them
across the wide prairie from beyond the feed lot.
How it felt to have arms stretched from their sockets,
the tingle of April frost fingers,
the slip, slap, of snow melt
against trousered legs.

I remember –
learning to save.
Dishes well wiped
before gurgle to hot kettlefuls.
Water heated on wood burning stove
in an oblong tin tub
used to bathe children by night light,
(all bubbles and laughter)
boil nappies by dawn-light in recycled water.
The hard white frost of washing hanging on the line
and how when summer came like a hot bolt of blueness
with its mobiles of bluebirds whirling above us,
I'd take a tubful of clothes to a sun-rinsed-wood deck
scrub out of doors
while chipmunk watched from the woodpile,
oriole from the birch tree.
Later, after hatch days, (as the sloughs dried)
mosquitoes, no-see-ums, wasps bombarded the tub
desperate for water and I'd have to retreat
sorry to leave a blackness of butterflies,
Mourning Cloaks dipping and sipping.

Now as burns rush down hillsides,
rivers flow full,
taps burst forth with unstoppered force
I remember a dryness of land,
the preciousness of water.

Margaret Gillies Brown

At The Pumping Station

An angle of empty land
amidst the fields:
the dry grass thick
with sage-and-pepper coloured
grasshoppers – living sparks,
flaring between our feet
as we cross the bridge.

The willows here are dark – no shadows left
only the soft wet gauze
of evening light,
and I'm thinking of the eels – those cords of thick
wet muscle in the grass,
crossing a meadow
and slithering back to the water.

I'm wondering what they feel, in the suck and flow
of powered currents, patterns in the mud
that never should have happened, how the thread
of nerve, like charged
live aspic in the spine,
adapts to each new tide
with supple love.

John Burnside

Rain

I am too old now and live in a busy place.
I cannot stand in the thunder rain,
let it slap huge drops on my flesh,
driving warm wetness
through thin clothing layers to my skin.

I cannot lift my head and hear the crack
of fat rain breaking on my teeth,
trickling down my throat,
sticking blackened rat-tail hair
to forehead and neck.

I no longer wear jeans,
to shrink while blue dye
runs down my ankles,
nor kick off shoes to
squelch muddy toes in sudden puddles.

But I can remember
and watch each drop
send its growing circles,
as the careless earth, stawed
by plenitude, repels the gift.

I can listen
to the rat-a-tat on shining leaves,
the drumming on the shed roof,
the hard spatter on the car
and wish I was in an empty space

where I could dance with the rain again
lie on wet grass, let it dissolve me,
salts minerals and soul,
driven in to the earth,
to nourish with the rain.

Janet Macinnes

Rain

The weather god wrings a watery revenge
on those who commit the sin
of having a right good time
so we took a hammering that day,
walking back from Shenaval. Rain fell
like I'd never seen before,
drummed on heads still thumping
from three nights worth of hangovers.

An Teallach and all his brood were gone,
lost in a deluge that turned the land
beneath our feet to mush; swelled
the stream in Gleann Chaorachain
to a cataract we dared to cross (taking
our lives in our feet as we inched our way
through the current's pull) – all of this
because of rain that fell and kept on falling.

That was years ago but I won't forget
in a hurry the sort of rain that laughs at gore-tex,
cuts you to the bone and chills
to the marrow. Hard to reconcile it
with the stuff I draw from the tap
or pour from a jug into my whisky as I sit
this evening by the fire while outside,
silently, inexorably, the rain clouds gather.

Jim Glen

Rapture River

1

How the mountain sits, sweats and toils
    As brown burn water
    Like eternal laughter
    Boils and falls from the hills
    Over moor, wet peat and belled heather

From where the white night-wind whets
        Its whistling whisper
    And spills its cruel chills
    Fiercely down into the river's meander.

2

    And yet again comes the rain
        The river in full flood
    Over the flat fertile plain.

    No refuge from the deluge
    No shelter in the delta

    Destroyed the entire terrain
        Suppressed that cry of pain.
    Water like a surge of blood
        Darkened by mud.

3

Hear that refrain of running rain
And that moan and sound
    Of an angry wind
        As if in pain.

    Claps of thunder
    Frightning lightning
    Signifying birth, earth, death.

Then that rush of air across anxious space
A hiss so great from the river in spate.

    The power, purr and murmur
    Of mysterious nature.

4

Relentless the waves so much deep water
Lying between them and us as the silver
Sky yawned and the clouds flew beyond

Over bridges to nowhere
As black skies opened and warned
That a land of the blind had been spawned

But onwards flows the river's dark water
Making each remaining structure
Shiver and shudder
Towards disaster

Where the abyss is endless.

Jack Withers

Reflections While Bathing

Gales batter the window with salvos,
Brassieres drip in the wash-hand basin.
I yearn for astounding twin rainbows,
Skylarks between them rehearsing duets.

A radio beyond my toes and bath-taps
Emits with smug urbane detachment
An interlude sonnet by Wordsworth,
Like Falstaff, babbling of green fields.

Rainbows and larks fail to materialise,
The Chopin recital resumes and my wife
Appears with a mouthful of clothes-pegs,
On tiptoe she appends a silk negligée.

"D'you remember that tune?" she mumbles,
Her profiled head and raised arms forming
A broken baroque arch with the mirror,
As she hums the theme off-key as usual.

"The Raindrop Prelude, what else?" I say,
As the panes weep and the mirror steams up.
I remember valedictory lines by Alkman,
A neglected Greek, mourning his youth –

No longer are my limbs able to bear me...
Would I were a keroulos, the sea-purple
Singing bird that over the wave's flower
Flies, having a careless heart...

Stanley Roger Green

The Ring

I spoke to him in Gaelic
A few words, like gold dust
Swirled from a Highland river, the last
Of an Eldorado that my grandfather
And his world possessed. It is enough
To make one gold ring about my finger
A marriage to a time that was
The last link before the rivers run dry
And the pure, good water
Stops talking for ever.

Kenneth C. Steven

Royalty

Like the great Inca,
who only wore a garment once
before casting it off, so
it is our privilege
to wear water.

We put it on (cast it off)
like a shimmering cloak; award ourselves
rhinestone crowns; ease ourselves
into the wrap of its clear
and perfect sheets –

while, elsewhere, a child stoops
over a hollow, glinting in the dry earth,
like a muddy brown slip
you'd step out of and leave
carelessly lying there.

Tom Pow

The Seahorse Sonnet

Let the faither the unborn bairns bield
bobbin in the balance o a bricht hoose sea
a new days daunce in kilter an licht field
skin shift tails twyne roond gress tae be
parallel promenadin in clean watters drift
Ayewies the couple in ocean trance daunce
ainly daith does a lifes allegiance shift
aphrodisiacs tae bring pleesure an chaunce
ainly lane horses dae lane horses find
awe the mair alane the mair open the kill
The twae backit baist lurches oan blind
the shy skin oan skin first feelins fill
touchin yer love in the deepest nicht
a bodys glow in the derk oceans licht

Harvey Holton

Seasong

Landlost with too much reason,
    almost defeated,
I long for the cry of passion;
I long for the white witch,
Her total caresses.
I long to bathe in her –
Wave upon wave
     attacking both body and soul.

The sea, my sea, surging,
        challenging
The land, white woman
Who exists in cool sanity.

So often life is betwixt and between,
Wavering so endlessly.
    Nervously evading choice,
Fear of hurt demands a pathetic loyalty.

It is all to do with land and sea,
The ultimate integrity
Challenging the coward in me.

David Morrison

Preparations For A Sea-Voyage

It was like this: we made the spare oars
from wax; the ropes from weed;
smoke we gathered into sails, and the prow
was once the concentration of a cat.

After the embarkation party the doors
and hatches were slammed shut and screw-locked
– yet gatecrashers and their girls, their relatives
and their girls somehow barged in,
promising to row.
We knew they never would. Instead
we forced them onto all-fours
to scrub the decks, the cannons, the cannon-balls,
the cabin-floors and holds.
We gave them mops, pails and promises of rum,
then left them.

In time they finished off their chores.
They caught and scraped sea-creatures clean
of phosphorescence.
(How the decks will shine at night!)
The mast, cut from the shortest distance
between two points sixty feet apart, they carved
and then inlaid with sea-tusk ivory
and oyster-shell.
New arrangements of shanties, jigs and reels
were made and photocopied for the crew;
they macraméd all the tangled ropes then neatly
lettered each one through like rock,
*"in memorium all those lost at sea
since Salamis."*
We expressed our thanks, suggested
they might form a chamber orchestra
or leave. They left.

When our automatic pilot tracked down
the setting sun we cut the anchor free
and opened more champagne.
And now – full speed ahead!
I fear these oars and sails will not remain
as oars and sails for very long.

Ron Butlin

Sequence

Deep as thought; dark as
a seer's eye; father of
rivers; of wishes.

Softer than kisses
lighter than laughter, your lips
chisel out caverns.

Smooth as sin; swifter
than hungry wolves; child-stealing
Dee each year takes three.

Abject beach, ravished
by the white-maned stallions of
the stampeding tide.

Jack Hastie

Shopping Trolley Detritus

shopping trolley detritus on the banks of Elvan Water   running snow melt
oxygenating sheep dip   forestry fertilisers   herbicides   fungicides
organophosphates   perennial reveries of sphagnums   of larch   of spruce
of petroleum itself slicked from the road   filtered through thin soil   over rock
mineral   of rubber & impacting metal death

clarity where
certainties end

a solitude of black
crows in the sun's fenced field

where breath is
tangible water droplets

through speech which
assembles disparity   diversity

(an apparent unseemly in
sensitivity a mere inability in
articulacy)

cut. diversity assembles
through speech

tumbling molecules of
water fallen syllables

let it go   no talisman against
this but breath   the
coughing heifer

yet here too the heron stands   she
stands her eye

ends certainty
where clarity

Gerry Loose

80

Lost Sister

As I tramp
through this forest of red pine
and juniper understorey,
with the taste
and stain of blaeberry
on my mouth,
I remember you.

The valley spreads
from three wooded glens.
Sometimes the cloud face
breaks into a smile
and I remember you
again.

There are places here
where you really would have smelt
the wild thyme,
heard stones chortling
in the burns,
and found pines
regenerating.

In the mountains,
where the ptarmigans
are rocks trundling away
on castors,
and where the mist
makes near look far,
you would have gulped the air
like spring water
into your lungs,
and felt your body surge
heavenward, undrowning.

This is the place
where our parents met like elements.
They made their commitment to it
and we were born from it,
from rock and water.

I have had my forty years
to learn the geology;
the five given to you
were a precious few,
hardly time enough,
I used to think,
to begin to learn the water.
While I have had the chance
to walk it all
with everything formed
to my advantage,
for you there was such a little drop
of anything: a melting,
a splash, an evaporation.

But the big river draws me
– as it draws all –
towards the roar and swirl,
of its kaleidoscope falling
from gravel beds and rushing white,
from boulder to knick
of the living rock it will mould
if it takes ten-thousand years.

And, as my eyes adjust
to the smoky water,
I see you again after all the years
distilled among the echoes
in a pool between falls,
a fish,
waiting for me to discover
what you have always known.

Douglas Lipton

Source

My friend Will tells me
that water has a memory –
the angle of the molecule
holds information.
So he says.

But I remember the light on the river –
river we called it.
The black peat water from the hills
is a dark burn flowing
through many years into the sea.

A drunk man gave me a bottle
and we drank the sweetheart stout,
fishing from the undercut bank.
The ancient eels in the black pool
tangled lines and stole hooks.

We're mostly made of water, Will says.
Which of us, he asks,
has not felt a yearning passion
for a river, for a loch,
for a waterfall. I don't reply.

Following the burn
on day-long explorations
looking for the source,
we came down from the hill
when the light was gone from the sky.

Later, not looking for anything,
but resting high on a mountain,
I saw a silver trickle running down
the face of the rock,
sinking into the damp black ground.

Our tongues taste shapes and angles,
Will says.
And when we drink
we taste the memories of the water.
I lick the wet rock. It might just be true.

Angus Dunn

Starfish And Capsicum

In my light room, the capsicum
sheds its fruit like peppery tears,
quietly wilts to crispy leaves and dies.

An old brick wall outside disentangles itself,
bricks, eschewing cement, separate,
sniff at the winds, sniff out the hills
and set off in a thousand different directions.

In a room nearby blood gathers in the cornices,
the walls sweat slime from sickly pores,
an old man in a chair in the centre of the room
possesses eyes which no longer function.

All of this I dream, see and feel:
I move away to a quieter place,
where the lips of the sea mumble
wordless and gumless at uncaring sand:

where a stranded starfish regards light as irrelevant,
yawns, stretches his many spiky limbs and
decides on a long slow stroll back to the sea.

Thom Nairn

Stolen Light

A shiver crosses Loch Stenness
as of thousands of daddy-longlegs
skittering on the surface.
In total silence
thunderheads close in.

Lead-shot from a blunderbuss,
the first flurries come.
The elements have their say;
the depths riven
as by some monster.

My inclination to run
hell-for-leather
lest this a prelude
to one of the Great Stones
clumping to the water.

A friend is writing
a book on poetry
and its inspiration –
brave man: imagine him
in flippers and wet suit

poised on the edge:
a charging of nerve ends
too rapid to track,
or underwater treasure
you hold your breath and dive for?

Stewart Conn

A Broken Surface Of Water

As soon as I reached
the Almond, it was
your face here
in ripple clear gestures
of this dancing river.

Thoughts are broken
by swallows through the air,
a murmur of laughter
from children fishing near
the deep waterfall pond.

Later, a downpour.
My poetry falls like prose.
Sometime I'll find a poem somewhere
perhaps when you recover
and I have gone.

Neil MacNeil

When Water Tasted So Much Sweeter

when water tasted so much sweeter
on my tongue and into my system
so much easier to catch than now
somehow, in the cells of a soul
baptism from within and such
a consoling flavour, taste, such
a taste at the back of my throat
so clean and free to breath, to swallow
to swim, to float at night right through
the liquid rhythm of dreams
and wake in the morning early
ready for the day to flow
and rush into it, waving, waving back
to when water tasted so much sweeter

Jim Ferguson

Swept Away

I remember the day
The sun went out
Floodwaters rose
And nudging debris;
You were there, high
Dry as ever
Your proffered hand
Just out of reach.
Alone, I clung on
Waiting for the fear to subside
Hell-bent on flight
The wrenching apart
Sounding
Echoes in an arid land.

Rosemary Mackay

Thocht Bi The Lochan

The gless o the lochan leims
an skimmers cannilie in the saur.
The splendor o the lift abuin
an the whyteness o the clouds
happin the taps o the bens
ir reflekkit back on thairsells.
A speir at the lochan: "Whaur can A finnd
oniething ither as claer an pure?"
"Anelie at the springheid o the wattir o life."

David Purves

Time Hurries Between Us

Time hurries between us,
like garrulous water.

There's a metaphor here
with a gossiping stream in it
full of blethering pebbles
and a rumour of fish.

But that runs between us too –
you on your bank, me on mine.

I could shout the inanities of love
and be drowned out by the roar
of the rapids of my desire,
but then you'd mouth back, "What?"

Instead I lean forward to ask:
"D'you want a drink, love?"

Time hurries between us
and I bridge it with the ordinary
words like "want" and "drink"
– and that rickety old word, "love".

Brian McCabe

Tumbling Cliffs

The cliffs are caught
in a stone tremble – a
slanting moment of change.
The sea, volatile pedant,
lashes and caresses
its argument into the land's
resistance. The bitten
apple with a bruised core
decays in the flash
of a thousand years.

Pamela Beasant

Uisge Beatha

At yir highest (some wid say)
tae cross the heids o weans an pray.

Tae tumble seaward fae great heights
an gaein by turbines giein us light.

Tae add tae blended but no tae maut,
tae tak yer ease in, fresh or saut.

Tae tease a troot fae, wi worm or flea,
tae wash yir face in or mak yir tea.

Tae bathe the wounds o wars unfair,
yi are the tears we cry sae sair.

Tae quench the flames o forest fire
but no the torch o oor desire

tae find the source o this wondrous stream
that gies us life an gars us dream.

Charlie J. Orr

Going down the steps
the sea

immense

engulfs me
in its big smile.

D. Zervanou

Uisge Spè

Nan d'rachadh agam
Air a bhith na mo mhiann rud
Fad dìreach ceithir uairean air fhichead,
'S e 'n rud a bu mhath leam a bhith
Nam Uisge Spè:
        Dh'èirinn ar á mhadainn
Agus gus do bheothachadh –
Theirginn a-steach dhut na'm ghloc-nid;

Nuair a thigeadh àm-lòin,
Chumainn blàths riut
Le bhith nam bhrot
Agus, às dèidh làimhe,
Dh'fhaodadh tu mo ghabhail nam bhradan-rèisgte
Agus, às dèidh sin a-rithist,
Nam thaghadh de mhac-na-braiche
Agus, às dèidh sin fhathast,
'S dòcha
Gun tumadh tu annam tiota,
Gus t'ùrachadh.

Oir tha mi cinnteach gun d'rachadh tu dha do leabaidh
Gu toilichte leam
        agus tha fhios agam cuideachd
Gun cumainn a'dol nam leum
Air do sgàth fad na h-oidhche.

Spey Water

If I could be anything I wanted
for 24 hours
I'd like to be Spey Water.

I'd get up at the crack of dawn
And – to liven you up –
I'd enter you as a morning dram.

94

When lunchtime came
I'd keep you warm
By becoming a broth
And afterwards
You could have me as a smoked salmon
And after that
As a 33 year old malt
And after that again
Perhaps you could dip in me
To freshen yourself up.

Because I'm sure you'd go to bed
Happy with me
And I also know
That I'd keep in spate
All night for you.

Rody Gorman

Rain Veil

The rain
beats persistently on the velux
Persuaded by an angry south wind.

This is my weather.
Unrelentingly wet; monotonously fierce.
Not miserable, you understand, or dreich
But the kind you hide from and wait.

Wait for kindness and gentleness
To re-enter your cosmos.
Wait for the sun to dry the chickens' backs
And evaporate the pools from your path.

If you could be a sailor
You could function in this fear.
No need to hang on for
The warmth and relative silence.

But you prefer to see it through
From the safety of your attic room;
The impenetrable screen of water
Bruising the roof slates is your protection.

With it you can do nothing.
Without it, the expectations are too high.

Siùsaidh NicNèill

Velasquez
(at the Edinburgh International Festival)

He turned the searchlight of his mind
upon each and every object equally,
persons or things as if each in its
difference, might through the precision
of line and paint, each weighed in the
balance of a mind, would yield
final truth, each equally capable of
telling the tale that words
could not articulate, telling
in the silence of the canvas –
the egg, the water in the glass,
the gourd, the features of the old
woman, the boy, the seller of water,
water of life he sold – that
crystalline freshness was his
to sell, to sell that which was
beyond price –
O SANCTUS SANCTUS SANCTUS
he heard the silent talk of the
star, and it became humanity.

George Bruce

For the begetter, Michael Clarke, of the Exhibition, *Velasquez In Seville*, at the National
Gallery Of Scotland, August 1996.
The references are to two paintings, *An Old Woman Cooking Eggs* and *Water Seller Of
Seville*.

Water

Water is,
often,
utter sparkle
and laughter:
and sometimes
it is
foam and froth
like the mouth
of a mad hound.

It slides
like a snake
around stones
and boats;
it is
invulnerable,
capable
of kindness and hate.

But I remember
climbing Cruachan
in a hot summer
and bending my mouth
to a cold cold spring.
It was heaven
forever.

And a world
without water
what would it be?
I carried
it often from the well
in two buckets
perfectly balanced
sixty years ago.

Calm water
where you can see
your face or a tree
or a mountain
or white clouds
passing so quietly
and smoothly
overhead.

Iain Crichton Smith

Watering

That summer my neighbour asked me to water plants
in his empty flat set tight under the hot tarmaced roof.
Each day I clambered up the wooden stairs that creaked
in the dry heat, and set the pipes snarling and choking
as water coursed through their veins again, and I
breathed the sweet queasy smell of damp earth
lifting from the pots and trays in a miasma of moist vapour
wreathing a world now different from the street outside.

The bright towels hanging limply in the kitchen
revived to taut fluorescent fabric ready to crack the air
with a whisk of the winds that might swoop from the porcelain blue
framed by the skylights, and their sweep of yellow ochre carried
a flash of beach as far as one could see through that slant door/
glimpse of rooms that my watering privileges gave me no cause to enter.
The slow drip of overfilled pots creating a winding Amazon
across the floor conjured up those night-time eaves

that drop private thoughts to each near-sleeper under rain,
and sent me to my duties in the roof garden. The snick of the hatch
propped against the chimneystack triggered the soothing rush
of city sound: water coursed from under the terra-cotta pots as though
the tree tubs themselves pumped the stream that revealed carbon black
        roof
under the summer dust. The water scent held the air fraught
with the promise of mist and spray: the tiny garden plots below
framed prospects of rain forest glimpsed from some pioneering plane.

My neighbour returned. But his holiday memories were not new
to me, with his long empty beaches and the tar-like smell
of endless waves under tropical storm skies. Long after
he'd fetched the next set of brochures (for mountains this time)
I remembered those afternoons of plants and heady vapour,
the slow-spreading strength of water.
I grew nostalgic for these holidays never taken.
My neighbour was puzzled by my moist-eyed reminiscence.

Hugh Macpherson

The Way

Water always finds the easy way
And it is the most beautiful way
Because it is the Natural way

Water always finds the noisy way
And water finds the silent way
Because there is a time for every way

Water always rushes the fastest way
And water crawls the calmest way
Because water Knows the only way

Water always flows in God's own way
And water falls in water's way
Because water IS
The Eternal Way

Alan McLeod

Blessing The Well

Source

Echo of nymphs and sprites
that cackle, curse and grow
will you flow sunk from sight,
or might the water-table rise
like indignation in the throat
and swelling swallow lies
in a flood of bitter spite?

Ceremony

Dress is suited to the garden party:
heads bound by hats, necks
wound with ties, starched chests,
corseted waists, seamless stockings.
We toast, champagne and chatter,
make sounds like rain on puddles,
the huge-voiced rock-thrapple
appeased with garlands,
sprinkled with sacraments.

Blessing

A light shower and we disperse,
vessels of the whale's fluted song,
the turtle's Atlantic yearning; wave on
wave of nursery years washes over us:
a mother's slaking benediction.

John Hudson

Wells

E lan wis set aroond wi wells
Each ane hed its name an story –
e puddag peel, Sanny's well,
e stroopie and e lairigie.
Twa skints o their watter now
wid rouze a gizzened spirit.

E spring far grandfaither took his horse
til bend her muckle lips and wi a kiss
crownkle a sepia mirror o clouds
is chist a hole in e heather,
chist a hole but some chiel fashed
til lay some bools for e beistie's feet,
a highway twel inches wide
til cool, din treasure.

A sweerie well, they ca'ad id,
ma fowk, fan in a summer's drocht
id dried, gied nae mair watter,
an they hed til fang wi frachts
fae some farrer source. Hard
work for bairns, e wecht
o twa lippin pails on a pole;
they kent e price o watter.

E lairigie – e farrest til win hom,
a mile or mair up ower a brae,
an halfway hom mayhap a tummel
an despair gushlan ower e gress.
Any watter wid taste sweet
efter sic a fang.

Each ane hed its name an story.
If ee could look far enough
intil their muckle deeps
fitna farlies micht ee see.

There's a clootie well near far I bide,
e shelteran trees festooned wi foosty rillanes,
a boorach o prayers an howps,
e moulderan fears o generations.

Wells arena chist for watter.

James Miller

Glossary: *puddag peel*: frog pool; *stroopie, lairigie*: names of wells; *skint*: soak; *rouze*:
drop; *gizzened*: withered; *muckle*: large; *crownkle*: crinkle; *chist*: just; *chiel*: man; *fashed*:
bothered; *boo*: stone; *beistie*: animal; *din*: brown; *fowk*: folk; *fan*: when; *drocht*: drought;
gied: gave; *fang*: carry a heavy burden; *fracht*: load; *fae*: from; *wecht*: weight; *lippan*:
brimming; *tummel*: tumble; *gushlan*: spilling; *ee*: you; *fitna farlies*: what wonders;
foosty: musty; *rillanes*: torn strips of cloth; *boorach*: mess.

Water Works

What works in water is its pull.
What we call wetting, flowing
is a force that sticks self to self,
self to other, other to other.

A grain of sand, cycled
from mountain to beach
and back, down again
to the surf's grinding

of stone on stone,
slips on a film
which smooths moves,
cuts corners, rubs roughness,

finds itself, dried, as dust.
Remember that sting on your feet
as the waves swirled grit
over your toes?

The moon-sucked sea did that,
as the fetch of the wind
tumbled surface imperfections
of the winter's skin

into waves, suspended grains
to hurl at cliffs, cut back,
blasted particles free
from their ancient matrix.

The backwash drags its load
of miniature gems – too common
to be precious; base prisms
where the sun is split –

and gravity layers the column
by weight of granules. An underflow
picks and lifts the specks,
and currents deposit them

in long up-slopes, and sharp downs.
Most dunes will last a tide, no more,
but some, it seems, exposed and buried,
dry and harden, fix their moments.

In the hills, slabs of quarry waste
display the ripples of an antediluvian sea –
holiday snaps from the Carboniferous –
and fossil raindrops where we ran for cover.

It's the same sand, from the start,
the same rain, the only sea,
the one water, indivisible,
first and final.

Colin Will

Scotch n'Watter

Pitter patter, Scotch n'watter
Mell as weel as cod wi batter
In this warld o win an weet
Hailstorms, rainstorms, snaw an sleet!

Scotia's weather's dreich an drookin
Paradise, fur sailin, dookin,
Hame tae salmon, trooties, eels,
Puddocks, kelpies, dyeukies, seals...

At brakk o day the kettles bile
Frae Thurso tae the Royal Mile
While coffee mingles wi the Tay
The Tweed, the Ythan, Dee & Spey.

Wee goldfish in their tanks at Troon
Frisk in their bowls tapped up wi Doon
In Inverness each font an ewer
Hauds Moray Firth frae sink tae sewer.
The yowes that sup the burn o Ey
Are blythe's the cheepin merles in Mey.
While tatties bile in special bree
At Kinlochewe frae Loch Maree!

In basin reamin wi the Clyde
A Glesga roader steeps his hide
Fite poodles, shampooed bi Loch Fyne
Pristine, cud at Balmoral dine.

Wi Firth o Forth Dunfermline grannies
Lather their pinkies an their crannies
While Embro bairns, wi jugs o Leith
Maun wash their lugs, their necks, their teeth.

The Gadie bathes, the Gairn baptizes
Fur salmon catch, the Dee wins prizes
While towrists read in foreign press
A monster lurks in derk Loch Ness!

Alang the Deveron, whisky stills
Pit mettle in the salmon's gills
While Irn Bru, frae Roosty nails
Is brewed wi bree that rinses whales!

Ay, H_2O rins throwe wir veins...
An oot wir taps an doon wir drains
Till Winter cams wi frozen pipe
That plumbers hae tae weld an wipe
Fin puddles dreep frae lum an ceilin
An plaister draps, wi paper peelin.

The thunner cracks! The lift grows dark
The doon-pish syne, cud launch an Ark
Toon gutters poor, like Blue-whale's spoot
It's weet eneuch tae droon a troot
Rain plaps on wellies, sypes on sark
Sends chip pyocks sweemin, in the park.

The self same rain that brews yer dram
That swalls the reamin Hydro dam
Daunces a reel at Burn o'Vat
At Loch Kinnord, lies douce an flat
On Ben a'Bhuird... a wreath o snaw
A fite carnation in the thaw...
WATTERS O SCOTIA, HERE'S YER HEALTH
THE WELLSPRING O WIR KINTRA'S WEALTH!

Sheena Blackhall

The Poets

Pamela Beasant was born in Glasgow but has lived in Orkney for many years and has appeared in several magazines and anthologies. Her collection *On Orkney* was published by Galdragon in 1991.

Sheena Blackhall has published many volumes of poems and short stories, mainly in North East Scots, known in that area as Doric.

Hamish Brown is the author of many books on Scotland, editor of *Poems of the Scottish Hills*, and a short story writer as well as a poet (*Time Gentlemen*).

Margaret Gillies Brown has published six collections of poems, most recently *The Footsteps of the Goddess.* Her autobiography is titled *Far from the Rowan Tree.* She was born in Edinburgh but now lives in rural Perthshire.

George Bruce is an Honorary President of the Scottish Poetry Library. He has published books on Neil Gunn and William Soutar and his *Collected Poems* is published by Aberdeen University Press.

Tom Bryan is a former Writing Fellow for Aberdeenshire (Macduff) and the author of two poetry collections. *North East Passage* was published by Scottish Cultural Press and *Wolfwind* by Chapman.

John Burnside is the author of six collections of poetry and a novel. *Feast Days* was published by Secker & Warburg; the others, including his most recent, *A Normal Skin*, by Cape.

Ron Butlin is a poet, short story writer and novelist. His most recent collection of poems is *Histories Of Desire,* published by Bloodaxe. Scottish Cultural Press published his novel *Night Visits* in 1997.

Angus Calder is well known as an historian and controversial journalist. His first collection of poems, *Waking In Waikato*, was published by Diehard in 1996.

Robert R. Calder is a critic, philosopher and prose writer as well as a poet. His most recent collection, *Serapion*, was published by Chapman in 1996.

Bobby Christie has worked with writers who are able and writers with learning disabilities. His published collection is titled *Transit Visa (N. W. Africa)*.

Tim Cloudsley is a poet and essayist who lives in Glasgow. His published collections are called *Poems to Light* and *Incantations from Streams of Fire.*

Ken Cockburn is currently Fieldworker with the Scottish Poetry Library. His first collection, *Souvenirs and Homelands*, is published by Scottish Cultural Press.

Stewart Conn lives in Edinburgh. His most recent collections are *In the Blood* and *At the Aviary.* He is co-editor of *The Ice Horses.*

Robert Crawford is the author of three volumes of literary criticism and four collections of poems, the most recent of which, *Talkies* and *Masculinity*, are published by Chatto and Cape respectively.

Robert Davidson is the author of two collections of poems. *The Bird And The Monkey* was published by Highland Printmakers in 1996, and *Total Immersion* by Scottish Cultural Press in 1998.

Christine De Luca is a poet writing in the Shetland dialect and English. She has had two collections of poems published by The Shetland Library: *Voes & Sound* (1995) and *Wast wi da Valkyries* (1997).

Des Dillon is the author of one collection of poems, another of short stories, and three novels.

Colin Donati currently survives in Edinburgh. His pamphlet *A Forest Seen Through The Belly Of A Dinosaur* was published in 1997.

Angus Dunn is the editor of Northwords. He was the second Robert Louis Stevenson Fellow and is much published in literary magazines and anthologies.

Colin Dunning is a concrete poet originally hailing from Greenock. His first collection is called *Contradictions* and is published by Arttm.

Sally Evans is the author of two collections of poems, *Looking For Scotland*, published by University of Salzburg Press, and *Millennial*, which was published by Diehard.

Gerrie Fellows was born in New Zealand but now lives in Glasgow. Her first poetry collection, *Technologies and Other Poems,* was published by Polygon. She was Writing Fellow for Renfrew District Libraries 1993–95.

Jim Ferguson lives in Glasgow and is the author of two poetry collections, *Strong Drink* and *The Art of Catching a Bus.*

Moira Forsyth has published both poetry and short stories. She received a SAC Writer's Bursary in 1996.

Pete Fortune lives in Dumfries. His fiction is widely published, and he received a Scottish Arts Council Writer's Bursary in 1995.

Bashabi Fraser is an Associate Lecturer with the Open University and lives in Edinburgh with her husband and daughter. Her first collection, *Life*, was published in 1997 by Diehard.

Kathy Galloway is editor of *Coracle* and a former co-warden of Iona Abbey as well as the author of several books. She edited the collection *Pushing The Boat Out* (Wild Goose) in 1995.

Magi Gibson was Writing Fellow for Renfrew District Council between 1992 and 1994. Her two collections of poems are *Kicking Back* and *Strange Fish* which she co-authored with Helen Lamb.

Sam Gilliland hails from Springside in Ayrshire, but now lives in Surrey. He is co-organiser of the Scottish International Open Poetry Competition.

Jim Glen lives in East Lothian and has had poetry and short stories published in many magazines and anthologies, as well as broadcast on Radio 4.

Rody Gorman was born in 1960 in Dublin. *Collected Faxes and Other Poems* was published by Polygon, Edinburgh, in 1996.

Stanley Roger Green is a retired Principal Architect of Midlothian District Council and the author of several collections of poetry.

Jack Hastie is a retired further education lecturer who has had a few papers in archeo-astronomy and some poetry published.

William Hershaw is author of *The Cowdenbeath Man*, poems in Scots and English, published by Scottish Cultural Press, 1997.

Harvey Holton has lived all over Scotland. His collection, *Finn,* was published by Three Tygers and his work has appeared in many anthologies.

John Hudson is a poet, critic and screenplay writer. He is editor of *Markings* magazine, and *Round About Burns*, published by Dumfries & Galloway Council. His published collection is *Medusa Muse.*

Kathleen Jamie is both a poet and travel writer. Her most recent collection, *The Queen of Sheba*, was published by Bloodaxe. She was Scottish/Canadian Exchange Fellow 1994/95.

Brian Johnstone is a co-founder of The Shore Poets and co-editor of *The Golden Goose Hour.* His first collection, *The Lizard Silence* is published by Scottish Cultural Press.

Helen Lamb's poems and short stories have been widely published and broadcast on Radio 4, Radio Scotland and RTE. Poetry collection *Strange Fish* (Duende) appeared in 1997.

Maurice Lindsay's latest poetry collection, *Speaking Likenesses*, was published by Scottish Cultural Press in 1997.

Douglas Lipton was born in Glasgow in 1953 but has lived in Dumfriesshire since 1977. He has two collections of poetry, *The Stone Sleeping-Bag* and *An Enclave In Eden* (nyp by Scottish Cultural Press).

Gerry Loose is a poet and editor and currently Managing Editor for Survivors' Poetry Scotland. His publications include *The Elementary Particles; a measure* and *A Holistic Handbook*.

Brian McCabe was Scottish/Canadian Exchange Fellow 1988/89. His first collection of poems, *One Atom To Another,* was published by Polygon. He is also a novelist and short story writer.

Ian McDonough hails from Brora in East Sutherland and is a much published founder member of *The Shore Poets*.

James McGonigal is a teacher of English as well as a writer. His collection is *Unidentified Flying Poems* and he has co-edited *New Writing Scotland* and *Sons of Ezra: British Poets and Ezra Pound*.

Janet Macinnes is a story teller as well as a writer of stories and poems. She has been widely published in literary magazines and received a SAC Writers Bursary in 1994.

Rosemary Mackay is a librarian in her home town of Aberdeen. Originally a short story writer, her shared collection is titled *Three's Company*, she has turned to poetry in recent years.

Alan McLeod writes poetry, film scripts and songs. His first collection of poems, *From A Gael With No Heartland*, was published by Scottish Cultural Press in 1996.

Anne MacLeod lives on the Black Isle, which she loves. Her first collection, *Standing By Thistles*, was published by Scottish Cultural Press in 1997.

Neil MacNeil lives in Sauchie, Clackmannanshire and is a widely published poet and reviewer. He is a creative writing tutor and former editor of *Strath* poetry quarterly.

Aonghas MacNeacail was Writing Fellow at Sabhal Mor Ostaig 1995–97 and previously at Ross and Cromarty. His most recent collection, *Oidheachadh Ceart*, was published by Polygon in 1997.

Hugh Macpherson was born in Edinburgh and has worked as a diplomat in Turkey and Brazil. He is widely published in literary magazines and is the fourth Robert Louis Stevenson Fellow.

Ruaraidh MacThòmais/Derick Thomson, born 1921 in the Island of Lewis, is the author of many books on Gaelic topics and seven collections of Gaelic verse, including collected poems *Creachadh na Clàrsaich/Plundering the Harp*.

Gordon Meade is the author of three poetry collections, including *The Scrimshaw Sailor*, (Chapman, 1996). He is a former Writing Fellow at Duncan of Jordanstone College and Dundee District Libraries.

James Miller is a novelist as well as a poet, *A Fine White Stoor* is published by Balnain. He was born and brought up in Caithness and uses his native form of Scots in his poetry.

Catriona Montgomery was first Writing Fellow at Sabhal Mor Ostaig and is the author of two collections of poems, the most recent *Re na h-Oidhche* was published by Canongate.

Edwin Morgan was born in Glasgow in 1920. His *Collected Poems* was published in 1990 and his *Collected Translations* in 1996, both by Carcanet.

Peadar Morgan is a Gaelic language activist and poet now living near Invergordon.

David Morrison lives in Wick, Caithness, is a poet and short story writer who is constantly, frustratingly, seeking God. He is editor of the magazine Scotia Review.

Hayden Murphy is a poet, critic and arts journalist and was editor of the broadsheet *Poetry, Prose and Graphics* (1967–78). His latest collection is *Exile's Journey*, published by Galdragon in 1993.

Thom Nairn is a poet and critic who has for many years been an editor at *Cencrastus* His second collection of poems, *Chagall Takes a Fall*, will be published by Scottish Cultural Press.

Siùsaidh NicNèill is a former Gaelic television producer and director, living on the Isle of Skye, and is the author of *All My Braided Colours*, published by Scottish Cultural Press.

Liz Niven is a writer and teacher, born in Glasgow but living in Newton Stewart. Her publications include *Ninian for Children* and she received a SAC Writers Bursary in 1996.

Gerry Loose was Writing Fellow for Glasgow City Council 1995–97. He is currently Managing Editor for Survivors' Poetry Scotland. Publications include, *The Elementary Particles, a measure*.

Charlie J. Orr lives with his wife and three children in Bonnyrig, Midlothian and is a regular contributor to various Scottish literary journals.

Janet Paisley is an award winning poet, short story writer and playwright. Her latest collection is *Alien Crop* published by Chapman. She received a SAC Writers Bursary in 1997.

Alistair Paterson is a poet, performer, and creative writing tutor living in Glasgow.

Tom Pow is the author of three books of poems, most recently *Red Letter Day* (Bloodaxe). He wrote *Royalty* while travelling through Africa.

Richard Price is curator of Modern British Collections at the British Library, London, and the author of four poetry collections including *Tube Shelter Perspective* and *Hand Held*.

David Purves is an environmentalist who writes in Scots and has had a number of scientific papers published relating to the recycling of wastewaters. He is a former editor of the journal *Lallans* and former Preses of the Scots Language Society.

Tessa Ransford was the editor of *Lines Review* for many years and is the author of several collections of poetry including *A Dancing Innocence*, *Seven Valleys*, and *Medusa Dozen and other poems*.

James Robertson writes poetry and fiction in both Scots and English. His first collection of poems, *Sound-Shadow*, was published by B&W in 1995. He is a former MacDiarmid Fellow at Brownsbank.

Cynthia Rogerson is a Californian domiciled in Scotland who describes herself as a "frustrated traveller immersed in domesticity". Both her poetry and short stories are much published.

Dilys Rose is a short-story writer as well as a poet. She is a past winner of the Macallan Competition and third Robert Louis Stevenson Fellow. Her collection is titled *Madame Doubtfire's Dilemma*.

Maureen Sangster was born in Aberdeen in 1954 and now lives in Edinburgh. Her first collection of poems, *Out of the Urn*, was published by Scottish Cultural Press in 1997.

Dan R. Skinner lives and works in Invergordon. He has had work published in NorthWords and animated poetry in the "Tricks Of Delight" exhibition which toured the Highlands in 1997.

Iain Crichton Smith is a novelist and short story writer as well as a poet. His *Collected Poems* is published by Carcanet as is his most recent book, the long poem *The Human Face*.

Morelle Smith teaches creative writing and lives in the Scottish Borders. Her third poetry collection, *Deepwater Terminal*, was published by Diehard in 1997.

Ian Stephen is the author of a collection of short stories and several collections of poetry, often illustrated with his own photographs. He was the first Robert Louis Stevenson Fellow.

Kenneth C. Steven has a poetry collection, *The Missing Days*, and two novels, *Dan* and *The Summer Is Ended*, published by Scottish Cultural Press.

Geddes Thomson was born and raised in Ayrshire, but now lives in Glasgow. He is a poet, critic and short story writer.

Valerie Thornton is a poet and short story writer. The editor of *Working Words*, joint winner of the TESS/Saltire Society Educational Book of the Year 1996, she received a SAC Writers Bursary in 1989.

Peter Whiteley was born in Yorkshire but has lived in Scotland since 1963. In addition to his poetry he has had a number of plays produced throughout the Highlands and Islands.

Brian Whittingham is poetry editor of *West Coast Magazine* and the author of three collections of poems including, *Industrial Deafness*. He was writing fellow at Yaddo, New York in 1994.

Colin Will is Librarian at the Royal Botanic Garden in Edinburgh. His first collection of poetry, *Thirteen Ways Of Looking At The Highlands – And More* was published by Diehard in 1996.

Jack Withers is a poet-performer who, as a German newspaper phrased it, operates in an area "Zwischen Gesang und Gedicht" – "between song and poem".

D. Zervanou grew up in Athens but has lived in Scotland for the last twenty years and is the editor of *Understanding* magazine. Her first collection of poems, *The Stone Moon,* was published in 1997.

Index

118